WONDERFUL
COMMON SENSE

by

JIM L. WINGROVE

HOW TO USE YOUR GREAT SUBCONSCIOUS

MIND WITH WONDERFUL COMMON SENSE

Jim L. Wingrove

Order this book online at www.trafford.com
or email orders@trafford.com

Most Trafford titles are also available at major online book retailers.

Printed in the United States of America.

ISBN: 978-1-4269-5907-3 (sc)
ISBN: 978-1-4269-5906-6 (e)

Trafford rev. 03/02/2011

 www.trafford.com

North America & international
toll-free: 1 888 232 4444 (USA & Canada)
phone: 250 383 6864 ♦ fax: 812 355 4082

ABOUT THE AUTHOR

I broke my arm in 1955 and had six operations. The bones were pinned with screws but the screws would not hold. So the surgeons took a piece of bone from my hip and grafted it to the broken bone in my arm and inserted a rod in the center of my arm and wrapped a silver band around it to hold it in place while it healed.

My Surgeon told me my arm would be paralyzed for the rest of my life. So I asked for an second opinion and the second Dr. gave me the same diagnosis. It was then when I applied Self Hypnosis in 1956 and since that date to the present 2010 my arm is completely normal.

Jim Wingrove

Contents

DON'T BRAG ABOUT WHAT YOU
ARE GOING TO DO

BRAG ABOUT WHAT YOU HAVE DONE

Jim L. Wingrove

ACKNOWLEDGEMENT

For the rare combination of drive, patience,
imagination, and zeal with which they served as critic
of each edition, I wish to express my appreciation, and
acknowledge my indebtedness to a wonderful group
who made possible the writing of this book . . . . .
EVERYBODY!

WONDERFUL COMMON SENSE

by

Jim L. Wingrove

IS MIND OPPOSITE?

Common sense will tell anyone that if a person would take the time to listen more, observe more, and *think* more, the wake of life for most of us would be more prosperous, more delightful, and more appealing than it seems to be at present.

For example: if being wealthy is your idea of life's fulfillment, then make it a point to observe closely any man of means – his mannerisms, his hands, eyes, expressions, the way he talks, the way he walks, the way he seats himself . . . . even go so far as to watch carefully the way he breathes. Check verbal expressions that he may use, watch the people to whom he may be talking, notice their reaction to such words as wonderful, delightful, nice, pleasant, or even the direct opposite of verbal expressions such as curse words. Common sense theory should tell you that every word, every gesture and expression has been, and always will be, a part of his successful way of life.

My theory of observation, along with common sense, to gain achievement is to use mannerisms, words, and actions to sensitize the brain of any listener for a period of time. May I make completely clear here and now that the words mentioned above: such as "nice", "pleasant", etc., spoken at a particular split second, will stun, numb, sensitize the brain, but only momentarily.

If only momentarily, to gain your listener's confidence, so that you may be able to sell yourself, your wares of propositions. This in itself will put you in full command of just about any situation, and in turn has started you on the road to success.

Basically, life is just the opposite of what you think it is. For instance, take love and hate – they are really very closely related, yet they are a direct opposite of emotional feeling. Truthfully, if you will admit to yourself any feeling of hatred you might have had for someone, there would be a strong feeling of love at one point, or the feeling of hatred would not have presented itself, in most cases.

There are also many people who cry at supposedly cheerful occasions, so we have sadness followed by joy.

If you will stop and think, I am sure you can make many things that are direct opposites, that will create instances with favorable rewards, even though they may seem ridiculous at the time.

Take for instance, a married couple having an argument. They may at the time seem close to hating each other, although the argument usually brings them closer together.

Now, let's take a person who is very ill with an exceptionally high fever, you would say when this fever had reached its climax, that this person is in his crisis. This is true, but it is also correct to say, once this climax is reached the person is well on his way to recovery. I will explain further. In the body the blood reaches a very high degree of heat, this in turn purifies the blood. Such as when you boil water, the germs in it are sterilized.

Another common thought: when vaccinating a person against polio, the thought would be to inject a serum into the body to kill the polio germ. Instead a live germ is often used in the injection.

A man is bitten by a poisonous snake, the common thought would be to inject a serum into the body to dissolve the poison; but by no means would the common thought to be inject a stronger poison into the body.

If a person is burned by fire, again the thought would be to apply ice water or something cold – but, no, it is the opposite. If a person is frost bitten, you do not build a fire to warm them. You do the opposite, apply cold.

Now, an opposite that you have certainly experienced.

Usually once a day, you must rid yourself of digested waste. If at this time you strain and push, exerting all pressure, you will probably end up with more problems than constipation. To rid yourself of this waste, you should relax. So, here again the opposite of the common thought. To prove the theory of relaxation instead of strain, that life is opposite from what you think. When a human dies, every muscle in his body relaxes and his bowels move.

Let's take something plain and common, something that cannot leave the slightest doubt in your mind about my theory.

Place your left hand in a container of hot water. Place your right hand in a container of cold water. Leave them there about thirty seconds. Now, place both hands in a container of lukewarm water.

You will find the left hand feels cold and the right hand hot. Just the opposite of so-called fact or reality.

I know a man who wrote a book about poor people, and it brought him riches.

The opposite of common thought has been proven in the pages you have just read. Therefore, it stands to reason, *man should think opposite of his desires.*

Still on the subject of minds, reaching into thoughts in the mind, there are schools that teach positive thinking, for example, to overcome a nervous condition, they will tell you to think the thought in your mind: "You are not nervous" . . . and to force this thought into your mind. When actually you should force the negative thought into the mind, and the result will come out positive. I will explain this in detail. Think a negative thought into the subconscious mind, so that the subconscious mind is aware of the ailment, etc. In doing this you are sensitizing the conscious mind. Once this is done the subconscious mind can then work with the conscious mind in overcoming the ailment or affliction.

For example, to rid yourself of smoking, think the thought in your mind that you are short of breath, you have a sore throat, and hoarseness occurs every time you smoke a cigarette. (This is applying the negative), and immediately as soon as you quit smoking all of the ailments will disappear.

For this, of course, you must make preparations, which we will discuss more at length in the next chapter.

Now we shall delve into the subject of when, how, and where to have thoughts.

First, let's look into the *when*: you must be completely relaxed, in a quiet and comfortable place – for instance, just before retiring or the moment you awaken in the morning.

A completely relaxes body will increase your power of concentration. Therefore, enabling you to think your thoughts more definitely into the brain.

How you present the problem to the subconscious is very important. Clear your mind of all other thoughts.

Then and only then should you begin to force the thought over and over again.

Remember, use a negative statement to achieve the positive.

Where should you think this thought? Naturally, you will say, in your head. Do you know what part of the head you should direct these thoughts to?

Scientific research claims there is a control point at the base of the skull that controls all thoughts.

In other words, if you have a thought, a desire to move your arm, the thought first goes to the control point. The control point then sends the message to move the limb.

Scientific research also tells us that there are certain groups of brain cells for each job to be done, such as hearing, seeing, or moving the arms, etc. Each has its own group of brain cells. Therefore, if the message is sent to the control point to move your arm, the control point in turn delivers this message to the proper brain cells, which in turn will move the arm.

What causes an individual to have a thought?

If the brain, for instance, has the thought, "go buy a pair of shoes," would you call this a subconscious thought? If so, what is the subconscious? Why wee you told to buy the shoes?

Why not a battleship?

This is called inborn instinct – when you are in need, your brain will instinctively relate to the proper brain cells, just what you are in need of.

It is correct also to assume what you think you are, is what you will become.

If it were possible to record every thought a person has, (meaning also thoughts you don't even remember thinking) – to record the thoughts day and night – day after day for a period of time, you would find that *the person is as he thinks*. In other words, if most of the thoughts recorded were thoughts of depression and unhappiness, then you would find that person to be, without a doubt, an unhappy person.

If happiness is what you want, force thoughts of happiness into your brain. This will eventually make happiness a reality for you.

THE TWO MINDS

How many of us have made the statement, "If I had my life to live over again, I would make many changes"?

I am sure with a little thought every one of us can do just this.

If I were to tell you that living over to make these changes is not at all necessary, *but that right now, starting at any age*, you can change your personality, increase your earning power, overcome all problems, or secure any desires, no matter how large, and that this could be done with very little time and energy, you would more than likely think this author was over-estimating the strength of his powers.

Nevertheless, I am making the above statement in the pages to follow.

I will prove each phrase emphatically to you, if you, as an individual will honestly believe, and completely cooperate with all experiments listed.

We know that each person has two minds. The conscious mind and the subconscious mind. They work together as a team or as partners.

Remember: One mind is of very little value without the other.

However, most of us go through life using only one of our minds at a time. Therefore, we reach only one-half of the desired results. Your conscious mind has an ability to release reasoning power, to carry out thoughts and ideas.

To carry them out in a proper and socially accepted manner.

Your subconscious mind hasn't any reasoning power to create limitations; therefore, the subconscious mind's work is to deliver the message to the conscious mind, so that it will be carried out in an orthodox manner. The subconscious mind will continually drive determination, and the will to do. Therefore, creating a capability to fulfill the desires to the most extreme limits.

Remember . . . . the subconscious mind is the boss. The conscious mind carries out the boss's orders. Exactly like a foreman must carry out orders from his boss, with discretion, perfection, quality, and speed.

Take this example: You have a desire for fame; you feel that leaping from a plane is the only way to achieve this fame – your subconscious, having no limitations to its desires, would allow you to board the plane, reach the desired heights, and then tell you to go ahead and leap.

Now, if you followed your subconscious mind's reaction to this fete, you would, in all probability, be killed. If your conscious mind is working properly with your subconscious, you would make careful preparations, you would don a parachute, checking it carefully, make your jump with perfection, floating easily to the earth, and be alive to receive your just rewards of fame. But, keep in mind, if you had not planted this thought of fame in your subconscious mind to begin with, the conscious mind would still have no desire to win fame; therefore, excluding a very valuable goal for your changed way of life.

Another example could be a mentally disturbed person; one imagining completely that he or she is a millionaire or a person of a certain type of character, such as Napoleon. This person honestly believes this thought, and acts it out to perfection. He is happy within himself because of his achievements; yet, normal people fully realize that this is insanity. They classify it as hallucinations or a wile imagination.

In all rights this is only one mind working, with all limitations of reasoning power gone. Even though the desire of the insane person has been reached, the sane person wants no part of this.

Therefore, rules and regulations must be followed, as well as the use of common sense. In order to keep a stable and socially accepted reality to your own capabilities before transmitting the thoughts of unreasonable achievements, that may well do harm to your well being.

Say, for instance, you feel that you are a complete failure in all of your undertakings; your desire is to be successful financially, and happy in all actions. Your desire for this goal is so strong that you have struggled, prodded, and racked your brain for years, as to how you can achieve this goal.

In all fact, you have tried, perhaps you have tried too hard.

In struggling toward this goal you have listened (and undoubtedly thought you were right), only to your conscious mind.

The conscious mind has been giving you ideas and ways of executing them, changing its motives and rules many times. This would naturally, keep your actions, thoughts, and labors going in circles, so to speak. This would leave you in a state of depression, with a feeling of failure and despair; with no desire to further your ambitions.

RULES TO OBEY

Study intensely, the following rules and regulations. They will teach you how to reach your subconscious mind and to return back to your conscious mind. For without a plan of operation, common sense will tell you there could be a danger in communications.

RULE I. Before planning a desire into the subconscious mind to carry out my desire, "I will never go deep into thought for any longer than ten minutes."

Remember . . . say this to yourself at all times before starting to reach the subconscious mind. This is a very simple rule, but very important in reaching your subconscious.

RULE II. Picture or visualize your desire at its utmost.

RULE III. When relating your desires to the subconscious mind, use a rhythmic pattern of speech, and always use the same rhythmic procedure.

EXAMPLE: Remembering you are thinking these thoughts to yourself: I will be happy. Over and over, again and again.

The big job is to get to the subconscious; coming back to reality is really quite simple in comparison.

Note: There are many ways of reaching the subconscious mind. I will now explain one simple method.

I suggest you experiment with your own desire or goal.

In explanation, I will use the idea or desire for financial success.

Get into a comfortable position, sitting up is the most desirable. Close your eyes and clear your mind of all thoughts. Meditate completely on your desire and repeat it over and over to yourself. *I will be successful.* Let no other thought enter your mind at this point, as you are trying to reach your subconscious mind. Temporarily your conscious mind should be inactive.

Continue this experiment for at least five minutes. . . . .repeating over and over again, slowly and deliberately . . . . *I will be successful.* Sooner or later it will connect with the subconscious.

Patience is a must when working with the subconscious.

We all know what anything worthwhile is either expensive, time-consuming, or requires hard work; so, naturally, common sense tells you that one experiment of this sort is not going to turn you into a financial wizard over night.

However, a continuance of this procedure several times a day will sooner or later succeed, and your desire will then become a reality.

Do not prod at your brain for ideas or suggestions, once you have reached your subconscious with your desire. The ideas will flow automatically with this procedure of operation. Your subconscious will form a mental picture and your successful future will fall before you.

Don't knock it 'till you try it! It will work! It is a sure thing! Many a successful man or woman will agree with me on this.

The power of the subconscious is greater than you can imagine.

Getting back to the subject of transmitting thoughts to the subconscious in unreasonable proportions:

Let us take a man, for instance, whom we will call "Mr. K." He had a main objective in life – to be a millionaire. He didn't care how he achieved this, nor whom it would affect; he didn't have any idea what the final outcome would be.

In other words, he had no plan of operation at any time in his mind. His only thought was to become a millionaire. He had no specific reason, no consideration for others, nor for his own well being.

Trying this theory of a thought without the thought of returning to reality, would be like a man traveling through a dense forest, knowing there is gold. But when he finds it, he also finds he made no plans for return. Which way is BACK?

In other words, he did not let the subconscious thoughts seep back to the conscious mind.

Therefore, he used his new found resources for greed, and undesirable endeavors, which in the end left him with unhappiness and disillusionment.

If this same man would have had a definite purpose for wanting and needing to be a millionaire, his first thoughts to his conscious mind would have been for the good this achievement would do for his family, friends, and his own well being.

He should have had thoughts of useful resource for his newly gained capital, and planted a vision in his subconscious of a self-made millionaire, sharing his wealth for beneficial reasons.

Then upon returning his desires to his conscious mind, he would start on the right road, and continue on the right road; living within the limitations of his goal and soon becoming a millionaire.

SUPERNATURAL

Things that are, or appear to be supernatural, is the topic for this chapter.

This may seem unnecessary to you, but as you read further you will see the connection of supernatural with good common sense.

Can thoughts be projected from one person to another?

Let us delve into the mysteries of childbirth.

You have naturally had children around you, either in your home or possibly in other people's homes. Children that are unruly, noisy and rude.

Were it possible to go back to the time of conception, and follow the pregnancy day by day, you would find the reason why this child is unruly and rude.

Let us look into the lives of two average women. The first we will call "Mrs. A.", and the other "Mrs. B."

Mrs. A. from the time of conception was happy, well adjusted, and had thoughts of pleasant things.

Mrs. B. was unhappy even before conception, and carried unhappy, depressed thoughts; her entire outlook on life and general disposition was that of gloom.

Mrs. A's baby, after it was born, was a happy, good natured baby. It ate well and caused very few disturbances in the life of Mrs. A.

Mrs. B's baby, after birth, seemed to have a sour disposition. It had colic, and the first few months of its life were constantly in an uproar.

In reading this, (and perhaps you have seen this happen) you can understand that when the supernatural or mysterious occur, it is possible to take it step by step and apply common sense to the occurrence. Thus, storing a *basic* knowledge for future use.

If, perhaps, for scientific reasons, a woman was situated in a room, isolated form all unhappy disturbances, from the time of conception; and all through her stay in this room she read, heard and thought nothing but happiness and goodness, -- thus transmitting happy thoughts to the unborn child – this would certainly have a good effect on the child; an effect that would stay with this child all through its life.

When the umbilical cord is severed, separating mother from child, would you believe this also separates the direct line of subconscious thoughts from mother to child?

To illustrate the unseen, the unconscious, the inner mind, look at what television advertisers do for advertisements.

They will flash an advertisement on and off the screen so fast that the conscious mind doesn't even see it. But, the subconscious does.

It registers in the subconscious and acts upon it.

Plainly and simply, you are what you think.

You become what you think.

What you are is a state of mind.

With deep study in this book, you will learn to create, in your mind what you want to be.

You can change your personality, your health, break bad habits, sharpen your memory, calm your nerves, raise scholastic marks, and instill self-confidence.

Anything you desire can be a reality. It is possible through wonderful common sense. Positive thinking, the will, hypnosis.

As the advertisement firms have proven, it is in the mind.

The mind can create health or sickness, poverty or wealth, illiteracy or brilliance.

The mind can be taught to think negative or positive, through hypnosis.

The proper approach to hypnosis can change your entire life.

METHODS OF HYPNOSIS

Hypnosis must be used correctly. When used incorrectly, it will do more damage than good.

The ability to hypnotize requires deep study, thought, concentration, imagination, a capacity to relax (complete relaxation) the mind and body, on the part of the hypnotist.

There are many ways to hypnotize. The style used on one subject may not hypnotize another.

Therefore, I maintain, there is no one that cannot be hypnotized when the proper method is used. A method that suits the individual, excluding, of course, the neurotic or those of an age that cannot comprehend.

Now, when I say, there is no one that cannot be hypnotized, I am speaking of the light stage of hypnosis.

There are only a very few, a small percentage, that are capable of going into the deepest state of hypnosis.

To induce hypnosis in the easy subject, almost any method may be used, such as the following:

Have the subject sit in a comfortable chair, in a quiet atmosphere.

Talk for a few minutes to the subject about sleep, and at the proper moment, when the subject seems to be completely relaxed, command sleep.

Another method which may be used, is, after situating the subject comfortably, have him gaze at a point about forth-five degrees above the level of his eyes. Continually talk sleep to him.

After about five minutes have elapsed, order him to close his eyes. You will continue talking of sleep; or, if the word suits the individual better, use "relax".

This may take fifteen or twenty minutes. There are certain times and individuals that require longer periods of soothing, relaxing talk. At these times it may take you as long as an hour to induce hypnosis.

If your subject does not go under in this time, he would be considered a difficult subject and a new approach should be used.

After getting the subject comfortable, have him count to himself, mentally.

Tell him to begin counting at one hundred, counting backwards by two's, such as: 100, 98, 96, and so on.

Tell him to continue counting while you give him his instruction of sleep and relaxation.

With a difficult subject you must speak rapidly to him. You must confuse the conscious mind. While, most important, you must command sleep at the proper time.

In the difficult subject, you should also use words that sensitize the brain: such as "pleasant", "nice", "wonderful", "delightful", and "beautiful".

This type of word will sensitize the brain momentarily. Even if you were to tell him in advance these words would sensitize his brain, when he hears them they will work in sensitizing and help you as the hypnotist, to induce hypnosis.

In confusing the conscious mind of the difficult subject, you could also try this method:

Tell him his left foot feels very cold and then immediately tell him his right foot feels very cold. Then back to his left foot. This time telling him that his foot is very hot.

Remember . . . . these words are to be spoken rapidly to the subject.

Another method used in inducing hypnosis, is to have the subject watch a bright object. A ring or a candle or anything that would be bright to the eyes.

Again you give instructions of sleep.

Have the subject continue watching that bright object all the time you are speaking the words of sleep.

There are times that a subject may go into a trance with his eyes remaining open. In this case, you may close them with your thumb and forefinger.

Very easy subjects may be hypnotized while they are standing.

For example, you may say to him that "by the time you reach the count of three, he will be sound asleep and that he will continue sleeping until you tell him he can awaken."

I might stress a point at this time also. The more intelligent the mind, the more susceptible the subject.

This is so only because the intelligent mind is capable of reaching the desired point of concentration, whereas the unintelligent mind's power of concentration is nil.

In hypnosis there is no danger to the subject whatever. When he is in a trance or under hypnosis, he is completely relaxed, so relaxed, in fact, that when he is left to himself he will go into a natural state of sleep.

I will try to relate to you now, what hypnosis is, and what happens to the subject.

There are three stages of our being: we have the waking state, the doze, and last we have the natural sleep.

The waking state is the period of time that you are talking, walking, eating, or the time when your conscious mind is alert.

The doze is actually hypnosis: so, when you are hypnotizing a subject, if you insert the proper words at the proper time (the time between wakefulness and a natural sleep), the subject becomes hypnotized.

And now you are probably thinking – everyone dozes. This is true. In fact, everyone does doze before going into a natural state of sleep. Actually you have been hypnotizing yourself since you were born.

After reading this, you can see there is nothing to fear from hypnosis. When hypnosis is properly used, it cannot possibly harm you.

You wouldn't drive a car, without first learning how. Neither would you fly an airplane, without first receiving proper instructions.

Hypnosis is a skill, an art which has been practiced since the dark ages. But before using it, you must study it. Learn all you can about the procedures and the use of it.

Hypnosis is reality. It is WONDERFUL COMMON SENSE.

It is powerful when you take the time and patience to study and prove out all theories.

Getting to know the human mind through hypnosis, is a tremendous asset to you. It can be helpful in almost any field of activity, such as:

Insomnia
Disturbing dreams and nightmares
Anxiety
Fears
Depression
Hallucinations
Sadism
Nervous Headache
Any nervous habit
Smoking
Drinking
Overeating
Shyness
Speech defects

and many, many more . . . .

When using hypnosis for any problem or desire, you must use the method mentioned before.

No matter what the problem or desire, *you must relax the mind, relax the body.* When this is accomplished, the problem or desire will be helped immediately.

I believe that the mind is like a radio, a sending and receiving set. There are certain cells in our brains that manipulate each part of our body.

For example: A person was frightened by something quite horrible. At the time this occurred, he jerked his arm. As it jerked it froze, or was stuck in a bent position. No matter how hard he tried to straighten out his arm, it remained in this bent position.

His conscious mind would not let this arm straighten. The cell that manipulates this movement was closed, so to speak, and would not open. The conscious mind was not capable of opening this cell; therefore, no matter how hard this person tried, he could not unbend his arm.

This person was then put under hypnosis. The subconscious mind took over, the brain cells opened and the arm opened as if it had never been frozen in the bent position. The mental block was broken. If the mental block is not removed from the conscious mind, upon awakening, the arm will again bend and remain there until the mental block is removed.

Now, let's get back to the art of hypnotizing.

If a failure to hypnotize should occur. it is usually due to the hypnotist's over-eagerness, or lack of concentration.

Very seldom will you find a subject who will immediately snap into a hypnotic state, even with a strong desire to be induced. Usually it will take some time to hypnotize them. Unless, of course, they have been hypnotized many times before.

You must take your time, working slowly, with adequate pauses between your commands.

Also, take into consideration, all disturbing influences in and about the room where your subject is situated. The sound of an auto in the distance, the drip of a water faucet, giggles from people in the room, a light that is distracting, any or all of these factors could spoil your chances for success.

You must be able to relate to him a realistic sense of sleepiness, while you issue commands to induce sleep. His imagination will make him feel sleepy even before the actual drowsiness overtakes him. This imagined repose brings him to the verge of the hypnotic condition you are inducing.

You must employ every means your own imagination can conceive, creating an atmosphere that will stimulate your subject's own imagination.

What your subject thinks is happening to him, actually will happen to him.

You should always consider the fact, that, you are dealing with intangibles. Nothing but mental power will achieve the results you are striving for.

Other than your self-confidence, your greatest tool in bringing the subject to a state of hypnosis, is imagination – meaning both you and your subject.

You must imagine that you feel, see, hear, and sense all that you direct your subject to do.

You must utilize your imagination to the fullest. You must imagine that your thoughts are in the frame of his body.

It is of great importance that you have confidence in yourself, so that you can instill this confidence in your subject. He must feel beyond a doubt that you will be able to hypnotize him.

EASY DOES IT.

STAY CALM AT ALL TIMES.

NEVER LET YOUR ANNOYANCE SHOW.

AT ALL TIMES YOU MUST BE DOMINANT AND COMMANDING.

YOU MUST SELL YOURSELF AS BOTH A TRUSTWORTHY INDIVIDUAL, AND AS AN ACCOMPLISHED HYPNOTIST.

One of the best ways to build confidences in others, is to have them observe you when you are hypnotizing others.

When they see the harmless methods you employ, and the respectful way in which you conduct the subject, through hypnosis, their fears will soon disappear.

Praise from your viewers, to their friends and neighbors, about your abilities will do far more in furthering your career as a hypnotist, than would any commercial advertising.

About the author: James L. Wingrove, his life and his time in the United States Navy. On December 7, 1941 I was Sixteen years old, my younger brother and I were in the movie theatre. The lights went out in the middle of the movie, and it was announced on the loud speaker by President Roosevelt that we were attacked by the Japanese in the Pearl Harbor. I knew then that I wanted to join in the navy. On September 4, 1942 I joined in San Bernardino. We were sent to Great Lakes Illinois for boot camp. Two or three days after my arrival, I came down with a severe food poisoning. I started getting sick to my stomach and then the next thing I remember is that I'm in the hospital and their pumping my stomach along with giving me a large glass of soda water. It was known that about one hundred sailors died from the food poisoning caused by the ham we had all eaten. It was later discovered that was how I developed diverticulitis which causes severe pain and also hospitalization a number of times along with bleeding internally and to this day I still have the problem. My family Doctor wrote me the following statement. Mr. Wingrove opinioned that he has the problem ever since he was discharged from military service and since he had a history of poison exposure while on duty. He believes that his diverticulitis is strongly related and linked to that incident. I believe that the past incident of poison exposure have been aggravating factors on his multiple recurrent diverticulitis, and may play significant role of the disease recurrences. Let's get back to Pearl Harbor which is now where I'm stationed and once again I'm on the ship with food poisoning, this time was not as severe as the first time. We reached Pearl Harbor on a weekend and there was a blackout. Japanese ships were headed to Pearl Harbor. We were not aloud to talk, smoke or leave our barracks. But were notified the ships decided to leave, so lights were on. In 1943 or 1944 another Pearl Harbor tragedy happened of which I have the tape of it can be purchases on the history channel. The other Pearl Harbor tragedy was where ships were docked side by side and one ship blew-up. And as ships were side by side the domino effect happened. I drove a motor boat going to my destination all I could see was one body after another in my path so I had to pull the boat fast left or fast right to miss the bodies. The other tragedy at Pearl Harbor was called The Wes lock tragedy. Upon my arrival to Pearl Harbor I met a sailor named Russ Porterfield of which we became good navy buddies. I spent three years in Pearl Harbor. I served in Cincpac, Commander and Chief of the pacific fleet Admiral Nemitz and served in Cincpac for three years. Anyway when World War II was over, my friend Russ Porterfield and I went on our separate ways. Mean while Russ tried for many years to locate me with no success. But finally he found me he got my phone number through the military and he called me and we talked and talked. We decided to meet in Las Vegas as you'll see in the pictures that are enclosed in this book. This was the first time we would see each other in Sixty years and to this day we talk often. My life after I got out of the service, well I bounced around working in job shops and I finally got a good job with the federal government with defense contracts administrator services where I worked for sixteen years. I was quality control rep. at the Downy office in California. I was strictly on the space shuttle for all my time with the federal government. Nearing the end of my life I was married to the love of my life I called her Miss Dottie. After I retired from the federal job, Miss Dottie and I spent our life playing bingo until she passed away. But I'm still a lucky man to have a wonderful daughter Sandy that looks after me and gives me lot of TLC to help me through my grief.

Mr. Wingrove opinioned that he has the problem ever since he was discharged from military service and since he had history of poison exposure while on duty He believes that his diverticulitis strongly related and linked to that incident. I believe that the past incident of poison exposure have been aggravating factors on his multiple recurrent diverticulitis and may play significant role of the disease recurrences.

Sincerely,

Electronically signed by:
EMANUEL BAMBANG KRISTIANTO MD
5/22/2010
3:02 PM
EMANUEL BAMBANG KRISTIANTO MD
Family Medicine Department
Southern California Permanente Medical Group
Temecula Valley Medical Offices
36450 Inland Valley Drive
Wildomar, CA 92595
(866) 984-7483

THOUGHTS BECOME A REALITY

THE MIND IS WONDERFUL COMMON SENSE.

The mind is powerful, more powerful than you can imagine.

Let us take the inventive mind for instance.

A few years back, would you have imagined that pictures, along with sound could be transmitted through the air, and into the box we now call television?

This was the mind at work!

A man had a mental picture of the television, and through a strong mental desire on his part, we now have a television set in just bout every home in the United States.

The same could apply to the new cars we see on the road each year.

Someone had to have a mental picture of this new styled body, a mental picture and a desire to transform this picture into a reality.

Many years ago, in the comic strips, there were men flying around in space ships, landing on the moon and visiting nearby planets.

At that time this thought was fantastic. It was completely unbelievable to most people.

But, because the idea was firmly planted in man's mind, the "ridiculous" comic strip is becoming a reality.

Take the building of a bridge: we know there is always a set of blueprints for a construction of this sort.

But, before the plans could be put down on paper, there had to be a mental picture, a dream in some man's mind of how this bridge would look when it was completed.

Now, let's say, the bridge is half done and the designing engineer is gone; he has disappeared and with him are the plans. Every set of plans that had been drawn up have disappeared with this man.

The bridge is half built and two hundred men are out of work because of this.

Naturally, the bridge cannot be left in this unfinished stage.

There will be some man with the desire and the will to complete this project.

Before he can begin his work, there must be a mental picture, a dream, a very strong desire.

Without this, the bridge could never be a reality.

If perchance the thoughts in man's mind were evil, by that I mean a thought that would not benefit humanity, this thought would not become a reality.

Have you ever wondered why, one child from a family of three children is smarter than the other two? Even though they were each given the same education.

Or, why one child from the same type of family, raised in the same environment, will turn out bad . . . while the others grow up to be useful citizens?

This brilliant or evil personality is created in the embryo. Thus, the mother's thoughts during the pregnancy had to have a great bearing on the unborn child.

Take a litter of kittens. One of the kittens is cuddly, the other one is mean. My theory on this is: while the mother cat was carrying them, her thoughts were transmitted to these kittens. Her unhappy thoughts were transmitted mainly to the kittens that, after birth, was mean and discontented. Her good thoughts were transmitted mainly to the kitten that was cuddly and content with life.

The thoughts were transmitted to the kittens individuality, this depending on which brain cell was active at the time. Thus, deciding which kitten would receive the thought.

Another theory on birth of opposite individuals conceived from the same parents is, the exact time of birth will have a great bearing on each individual's personality.

By this, I mean, at 6:00 A.M. the temperature, the atmosphere, the particles in the air, all will have a part in creating individual personalities. By 6:00 P.M. they have naturally changed, creating an opposite in personalities.

COLORS IN OUR LIVES

Certain colors have an effect on the brain. For example, if the color yellow were put before an individual's eyes, the color (yellow) registers in the brain, which produces a feeling of happiness and joy. This happens automatically as soon as the eyes make contact with the color.

However, if the color red is placed before the eyes, a feeling of distress would register in the brain. Each and every color produces a different registration of feeling when it is registered in the brain.

The above isn't just theory. It is fact, as stated in a popular magazine.

I maintain that a person could be treated by color therapy; take for example a person suffering from a nervous disorder. It would be necessary first to determine which color has the desired effect on the person's brain; and this can, of course, be determined proof-positive by connecting the electrical machine directly to the brain, as was explained in detail in the popular magazine. Now, once the color is determined for the particular ailment with which the person is afflicted, the color therapy could begin.

For instance, if it is determined that the color yellow is the proper color, then the subject would be placed in a room which is painted yellow-walls, ceiling, floor and every object in the room must be yellow, including lamps, bed chairs, etc; even the light fixtures and light bulbs should be yellow – not one single object in the room should be of a color different than yellow.

Now, the subject should be confined in the room daily for approximately one hour. The number of days the therapy would be required would depend upon the condition of the subject.

Further, with color therapy, hypnosis should be injected to the person - - - not in person, but piped into the room via radio, etc. It is very important that for the full hour the subject must keep his eyes open, gazing continuously at the yellow color (do not stare).

Also, the room should be filled with a particular odor. Again, the particular odor should be selected for the particular ailment. For instance, the odor of burnt toast or the smell of garlic or the smell of crude oil, or even the smell of rotten eggs. The sense of smell is very important in hypnosis, as different odors have different effects on the brain and the subconscious. The sense of smell has been ignored in scientific research to a minimum as to effect on the brain cells.

The author would like to revert once again to the subject of the importance of colors in our lives. I believe colors could be one of the most important governing factors in our lives.

For example, colors which surround us daily could control our thinking, and further determines the condition of our bodies, specifically, whether we are well or sick; and even to the type of illness we may acquire, whether it be cancer or gallbladder trouble.

Substantiating my belief that colors have a great effect on our lives, particularly the color of our clothing has a great effect upon us, since we know the sun's rays draw differently from the color black to the color white.

This is also true in all colors which surround us: the color of our house, the color of our furniture, our car, and even the major colors in a town which a person drives through daily.

As a matter of fact, we seem to subconsciously stick to certain colors. For example, you've probably purchased a car, having in mind before you go to the dealer that you want a white car. But when you get there, many things are involved, such as, does the motor run good, is the condition of the car good, etc.? My point is: you will doubtless buy a blue car, or some other color, -- not the white one you originally wanted; and again, you are stuck with the colors which surround you daily. . . . . and have surrounded you since the beginning of your life.

You probably know someone who had bad luck all of his life, and he moves to another town and all of a sudden, this person seems to click. Now, remember, the colors in the new town are probably different.

As another example, you probably know of a cafe where the owner made a good living for a number of years, then he sold it to a new owner. The new owner just can't make a success of it. Could it be that the new owner in cleaning and painting the cafe, changed the whole color scheme.

It is my opinion that more research should be made in this field for our own health and welfare.

North, East, South or West? Or, have you ever thought of which way you face at night when you sleep? Which direction your bed is facing – North, East, South or West? Does the way your bed is pointed make a difference whether you are a success in life, or even make a difference in your personality. Or perhaps, typing all together, the way you face *most* the greater part of your life; meaning: when you talk to people, say standing at night, which way are you facing.

How is your furniture arranged in your home or at work? Or, even to which way do you face if you go out to eat at that favorite cafe? Does the way you face most of the time control, perhaps, your personality, your health or success in business; or even controls how many friends you have.

So, if your luck has been bad all of your life, CHANGE YOUR DIRECTION.

Yes, if you are in your 30's and you don't have Five Thousand Dollars in a savings account, then I am telling you now it's *TIME FOR A CHANGE*. It's time to look yourself in a mirror and say to yourself: that what you are is not very much and nothing much to be proud of. So you must start doing something about it. *IT'S NOT TOO LATE!*

Start by becoming aware of yourself, being aware of your actions; being aware of the daily habits you've fallen into; become aware of the following:

a) Which way are you facing when you talk;

b) Which way are you facing when in bed?

c) Which way are you facing most of the time when sitting in your home; also, at work?

d) Also, if you spend a lot of time with friends, note the direction you are facing while sitting or standing.

Next become aware of the colors that surround you daily (meaning at home and at work); the color of your car; the color of your clothes. Even become aware of the color of your favorite coffee cup, of dishes; even the color of the food you eat daily.

Next if you wish to change your life, become aware of the way you breathe while at work, at play; the way you breathe at home; at friends; driving in traffic. Become aware of the way you breathe – whether fast, or perhaps you breathe in a rhythm. Do you generally breathe deep, or do you take short breaths most of the time? How about while you are asleep – how do you breathe?

Next, become aware of the way you speak.

When you talk to people do you run all of your words together, or do you pause between words; do you talk slow or fast; do you talk loud or very low and soft when trying to sell or get a point across?

I say again: become aware of everything that exacts around or concerns you.

I suppose by this time you are saying to yourself "I am now completely aware of myself now that you have brought all of these things to my attention." Well, I can tell you right now that you are mistaken. You are still not completely aware of yourself.

How about sounds that surround you daily?

I am talking about the dog's bark, a car's horn, a train's whistle, the sound of an airplane.

I am saying here and now that sounds that come into your ear daily – all kinds of different sounds you hear daily register different emotions in your brain, and this in turn, governs your life. Add to that sound is one of the governing factors that might be governing your life of health, wealth, happiness or success.

I'll repeat once again: become completely aware of yourself, and health, wealth, happiness and also success and *without any shadow of a doubt* will become exactly your desires.

But since I've added the last subject, I am telling you now that you are still not aware of yourself completely – and which you must be – before you will ever satisfy all of your desires.

All right, now here is another factor which without a doubt you are not aware of: How about when you sit in a chair while visiting a friend, or when you sit at work or sit in a movie theatre – when you rise (or let's say "get up"), *which foot do you move first*? Is it the left or right foot that raises off the ground (or floor) first? When talking to a person, which hand do you move trying to get a point across? Such as for instance, pounding the table; in other words, which hand moves the most while trying to get your point across. Again, this would be a governing point, of what reaction this registers in the brain, which again helps determine your desires.

And this another factor for your consideration: THE TOUCH! During the day how many different emotions are registered in the brain? By touching a person's hand, for instance, a person when you secretly care about, registers your desires. Or, let's say the touch of hot or cold, smooth or rough, or pain? Or how about touching something that is nasty, such as changing a baby's diaper and you accidentally touch the waste in the baby's diaper – now which way does this register to the brain? Does it register for or against the desires wanted? Or, how about touching someone you dislike.

Here is another very important governing factor that might control your destines – *THE SMELL*. How about the smells that surround your daily life? Do you live next to a glue factory or next to an oil refinery or a bakery? Each different smell registers different emotions for good or bad, whether the smell is pleasant or a stinking smell. How about the smell of, let's say, paint smelled daily – would this register to the brain to grant your desires or would it register against your desires?

So, I am telling you *that you must become aware that you are aware of everything that touches your life.*

CONCLUSION

When we figure out the key to the mind, and there is, without a doubt, a key, then all mankind will reap the benefits.

I am not saying here, that the key has not been found. To the contrary, I believe it has been found.

It has been found by our inventors, the inventors of the electric light, the telephone, the atomic bomb; by poets, by artists, by great athletes, prophets and writers.

May I further state, it is my theory that Jesus Christ found the key to the mind. That he was the master of all masters. That he was the only one of all beings to master the art. He, Jesus Christ, was in my opinion, a hypnotist – a master at it.

To master is perfectly – that is a thought to think about.

Now, until I hear from you, and I will,

"THINK A THOUGHT IN YOUR MIND!"

James Wingrove's view on Politics

In reference to this letter I wrote an sent to the Press Enterprise newspaper printed in the opinion section on August 6th 2009,and that has a very high volume of circulation. The article reads; "Fix budgets Now." Our Representatives let us get into this terrible and powerful nation again. We need a fix Now, not in two years or moer. If all Representatives, state legislators, governors, members of congress, senators and state officials would work for 50 cents or zero pay for two months, I believe it would turn this country around and put us back on our feet again.

Fix budgets now

Our representatives let us get into this terrible, devastating mess that we are in today! We hired all the representatives, to put everything in order and make this a successful and powerful nation again.

We need a fix now, not in two years. If all representatives, state legislators, governors, members of the Congress, senators, and state officials would work for 50 cents or zero pay for two months, I believe it would turn this country around and put us back on our feet again.

JAMES WINGROVE
Quail Valley

THE CALIFORNIAN
COMMUNITY VOICES
2010

Fix budgets now

Our representatives let us get into this terrible, devastating mess that we are in today. We hired all the representatives to put everything in order and make this a successful and powerful nation again. We need a fix now, not in two years or more.

If all representatives, state legislators, governors, members of the Congress, senators, and state officials would work for 50 cents or zero pay for two months, I believe it would turn this country around and put us back on our feet again.

I sent this to President Obama and his reply was, "It will take two years or more." My reply to him is, "Simply answer my question: Will you all work for 50 cents or zero pay for two months, or do you want to keep all of your money?"

JAMES WINGROVE
Quail Valley

This was in 1942. Russ and I were both 17 years old.

Jim and Russ met in Las Vegas in June 2006 This was
the first time we seen each other in over 60 years.